Windows 10:

2019 Updated User Manual with Everything You Need to Know About Windows 10

ISBN: 9781099977497

CONTENTS

Thank you for purchasing this book!

We always try to give more value then you expect. That's why we've updated the content and you can get it for FREE. You can get the digital version for free because you bought the print version.

The book is under the match program from Amazon. You can find how to do this using next URL: https://www.amazon.com/gp/digital/ep-landing-page

I hope it will be useful for you.

Introduction

Windows 10 has changed the way Windows OSes work, and it is important that you know how to use it. With the correct

4

understanding and usage of this system.

Windows 10 has changed a lot of people's experience with Windows OSes, which in the past has not always been that great. But, this one streamlines all of this, making it possible to use no matter who you are. If you are someone that's struggled with Windows 10 in the past, or maybe you have decided to finally upgrade, here we will tell you everything that you should know.

In addition, it is not just going to be the new features either. We will walk you through how to navigate some of the big parts of Windows 10, and some key features that Windows 10 has that other systems may not have. There are a lot of cool, new things that you can use in order to truly get the most out of Windows 10, so if you have been curious about some of the benefits of Windows 10, well you are in luck. In this, we'll tell you everything that you need to know about Windows 10, so that you can get a better, more rewarding result from this, and one that can help you truly get the most that you possibly can from a Windows system. So what are you waiting for? It is time to learn all about the features of Windows 10, and how these can help you use the system even better.

Chapter 1 – The April 2019 update, along with Build 18362

First thing we will discuss is the big April 2019 update, which actually did not happen. Instead, it is now the May 2019 update, which is available now. Whoever, lots of people call it the big 2019 update since it has changed the recent was supposed to have some major updates that were instead, thrown into build 18362. But, we will touch upon all of these, and why the matter.

The Improvements

With the so-called April update, it actually was planning new features, and improvements that came from refining the interface. The changes were supposed to be I the sign-in screen, which had an acrylic background that allows you to focus on signing in as the controls are now up towards the higher end of the visual hierarchy. Yo9u can get the acrylic effect, and it does make it clearer. It also changed how clear it was to navigate the start menus, such as icons that would change the way you start, sleep, or shut down the computer, along with the start menu appearing as a separate process. It also did get some Windows defender improvements in order to help people have better security, and it also has changed some features for Edge users that want to manage the microphone, along with the camera when they choose to browse.

But, this feature has been actually paused, and it users are happy to wait. That is because Microsoft understands how annoying these updates can be, since they put your computer out of commission. You can actually, with the now may 2019 update, choose when you want to update your systems. That is important, because who actually wants to sit around and wait for an update. It is definitely something that people e can benefit from, since they do not have to deal with this during work hours.

So what is in Build 18362?

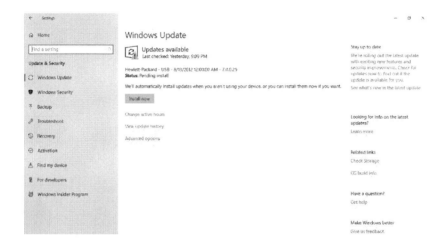

As we have stated before, this is the official name of the May 2019 update, and there is a lot with this. For example, as we have stated before, the new sleep, shut down, and restart icons are clearer than ever, and you can actually change your account settings sign out, and lock in the profile menu. You also may notice that the start menu looks clearer. Too, and it does simplify the debugging and the isolating that happens with users when they use this service.

It also comes with a light feature, and this is a light desktop theme, which is basically the opposite of the dark mode that you already have. This makes the start menu look lighter, but the icons also have been created to fit the theme, so it looks a lot lighter. Basically, if dark ode is not your thing, this is a different way to approach this, since it does allow for you to get the most that you can from this, and in turn, create a better, more rewarding experience with your Windows machine.

The Edge Browser has also changed as well. This gives you a

chromium based one. Edge has been struggling for years, but this may be the solution. Chromium based means that it is open sourced, and it is compatible with the popular plugins and websites. This one also has the internet explorer mode. This is a good one that fixes the problem for those who like internet explorer, but they don't' want to deal with the browser restrictions. This also contains some new privacy options, the "fluid framework" for developers in order to get a better and more interactive experience enhanced by the AI, along with collections feature that allows for people to organize, collect, and then share the content from all around.

There is also a specter fix. This is actually a design flaw that is in CPUs that allows programs to escape the restrictions that are there, and it will read the other memory spaces on programs. Microsoft noticed this, and they actually patched Windows in order to block these attacks, and it actually has helped, but in some cases, it has affected the speed in some cases. But, with the new April and May 2019 updates, it actually has sped your PC back up, and it has enabled import optimization and retpoline as well. It will make your PC faster, and you will not even need to think about it. That is so cool!

Cortana has also changed as well in a couple of different ways. First and foremost, Cortana isn't in the search bar, and that's something that a lot of people like, because sometimes they don't' want to have to accidentally press the button. It splits up Cortana, and settings has also been split up, along with the group policies, so that when you click search, you get literally a search. Your'e not summoning Cortana every time anymore, and you can use the separate icon for this.

Cortana is not just away from the search bar though, she is also smarter. That is because of the recent acquisition that they had with semantic machines, which helps to build a new and better AI technology straight into Cortana, providing helpful, more sophisticated answers, rather than bad answers to the queries that you have. Cortana will actually get previous information if you have that in order to suggest other information to help you. Basically, Cortana has learned how to be even better with information than before.

The biggest change: updates

Finally, it handles the issues with storage that the original Windows 10 updates have not fixed. Lots of times, when you have updates that don't install properly, it's because there isn't enough disc space, and on inexpensive devices, they either are screwed because they don't' have space of it, or something else. But, there is a chance that now, with the update, you can fix that. The space that is here can be used solely for Windows updates and temporary files. When Windows needs that space, it will delete and perform, so the space is not totally wasted, and it is definitely a nice addition to Windows 10, especially for older devices.

But that is not all. This one actually can also allow you to pause system updates for a few days. This gives you some breathing room for when you need to put the update in, and if there are issues or whatever, you can pause the update till it's fixed. In a perfect world, there would not be issues, but if your'e someone that does not feel needs to update all the time, this may be a good one for you.

Windows 10 has changed the name of the game with all of the different changes that you can put on this. With all of these added, ti's no wonder why people are flocking to it these days, since it's worked to actively change the process so it's less of a hassle, and better for you as a user.

Chapter 2 – New Windows 10 features to try out

Windows 10 comes with some awesome features, but what is so good about them? Well, read on to find out. Here are the new recent features that you can get with Windows 10 that you will not get with other systems.

Copy and Pasting Photos from Clipboard and Phone

This was from the 2018 update, but you can use the cloud-based clipboards in order to copy along with pasting images from a PC to another. You go to start, and then choose settings and then system, and then clipboard, and from there, use the toggles to turn on the clipboard history, along with synch across devices. You can also use your phone app in order to see recent photos and text messages from the android phone. By dragging this from the phone app to an email, or whatever, you'll be able to use it, and it makes sharing pictures and such so much better, and so much easier.

Windows Sandbox

Windows Sandbox is something that may be interesting for those that are running on the professional software. This is something that is currently available because of the May 2019 update, but it also is something that allows you to run virtualized types of Windows 10 software, and it allows you to test out code and settings without affecting the original installation. If you're curious about this, especially if you're a programmer, then you'll definitely want to find out more about this, since it can change the way your coding works.

Passwordless Accounts

This is something that, if you are curious about this, you may want to try, but it does bring about security concerns. It is a new Microsoft idea, where they run a "world without passwords" where you can create a Microsoft account without a password, and it's linked to the phone number, and you'll get a security code when you log in, which might be cool if you are considering this, but it does bring potentially new concerns for security to the table, but then again, for some people, if they hate remembering 20 different passwords, this might be a good investment.

More Windows hello Options

For some people, they may want to sign in from different areas. The sign-in options can be accessed within account settings and they are grouped in a compact, simple-to-read format, and once you click on any of these options, you can expand it, and then set up the settings changes. You can also put a personal security key on this as well for extra protection, so you are getting some new ideas and features with this, and if you want to enhance your sign-in options, this is how you do it.

New Font Installer

This is something that has been a problem for Windows systems for a long time. Font installer is something that has been a part of Windows systems for a while, and it needs a new look to it this is actually a drag-and-drop font installer that is at the top of the settings, personalization, and the fonts page. It is super easy to use, and if you see the font's preview on this list, you will be amazed at how helpful this can be, and it allows for a better, no more noteworthy system that can help you get the most out of your Windows system that you can.

New Emojis

If your'e someone that likes to use emojis, whether it be on Windows systems, or mixed with your smartphone, this is a great one. This is something that has been a part of the text fields on Windows 10 systems since the 1709 update, and when you press the Windows key, along with the period, or the semicolon, you can actually choose from a list of emojis. You get two new emojis with this, which are emojis, which are character-based symbols, and symbols that you can use for apps, such as Character Maps. You can now enter inverted question marks, or the interrobang without needing the alternate keyboard, or even ASNI codes, so it is changed the way you navigate Windows 10 forever.

Uninstalling Apps

This is a feature that Windows 10 has been continuing to work on.

Windows 10 lets you uninstall those built-in apps that you do not need such as my office, along with Skype, but it also will let you uninstall Groove music, 3D viewer, Music, Mail, Paint 3D, and other ones. While it does not fully extend to all apps, such as Edge browser and the store app, it will allow for you to remove most of the apps that you don't want.

Magnify the Screen

This is a good one for those who would like to improve their usability experience because the screen is too smaller. This is an enlarger that allows you to make the words and images simpler to read. By pressing the Windows logo key, along with the plus sign, you can magnify this. If you want to remove it, it is that simple too. You press the Windows logo key, along with the escape key in order to return to the original size.

Windows insider Perks

If you are someone that uses Windows insider, expect new benefits. There used to be the last ring, and then the slow ring, but now you have the release preview ring, and the option to skip as much as a year ahead into your building cycles, and it also allows you to opt back into the mainstream when you finish the current cycle, and it will allow you to get a redesigned settings page as well. You click current settings, then current ring, and from there, you are done. If you use Windows insider, this is a great feature.

New Screen Capture

This is something that has been around, but now it is called nip & Sketch. This is something that mac users have had the pride of having, but Windows has recently changed this. While most don't' realize that you can capture with Windows plus Shift plus S, you can actually use this to store your captures into a PNG file. This allows you to see the history of this too, and synch it up to the same account with the cloud system. This also lets you mark up screenshots with a so-called digital pen, and it is in the lower right corner to help you with your inking capacities. It is a great feature for those looking to make sure they have the best possible screen capturing tools, and it does rival MacOS Mojave's.

With Windows 10, you are getting new and improved features, and as you can see from them, you are getting features that can help you as a user, so that you can get the most out of your system, and to help make it worth your while.

Chapter 3 – Multitasking customization with Windows 10

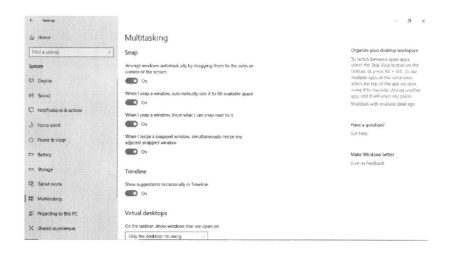

Did you know that you could multitask in Windows 10? You may wonder why you would even consider this, but think about it, if you are going to be using Windows 10- for a lot of things this is something that can ultimately help; you get the most that you can from this. Here, we will be discussing how you can manage different Windows in Windows 10, along with why this might be something to consider in Windows 10 period.

Snap it

Snap and Snap Assist for Windows 10 are both really good

options, especially if you have multiple apps open. In order to snap a Window, all you have to do is drag the top of the Window itself to the side. This then will come in to help you figure out what apps you want to snap into in order to provide more spaces for your screen. You can also snap apps to any of the corners that are there by dragging the title bar of these to the corners. It is a great and efficient sort of system, and it makes a huge difference.

Task view

This is an alliterative to the Alt+Tb option that has been around for a long time. While it is good for letting you switch from different tabs, such as the next and previous one, if you have a lot of Windows open, such as 10-15 of them, you are going to find out that this can be a bit of a nightmare. Task view is the alternative to this, and it will help with making the size of the text at least manageable to read. It will give you a graphical view of every single open tab that is there in the zoomed-in rectangle preview of the Window, and from there, you choose the one that you want to switch to, and it will switch it instantly, making it a lot easier for you to deal with.

Virtual Desktops

This is a great one for if you do not have a second monitor, but you would like to multitask with many different apps. It allows you to see everything, and you can run multiple apps that the display is able to handle. However, not everyone is really gearing towards that second display, but if you're someone that likes to have a laptop, the secondary monitor isn't going to work for you, so you need virtual desktops, which essentially allows you to create a number of desktops, and you'll get access to the start menu, taskbar, and the like, and you literally do this by pressing task view on the taskbar, or Windows and then tab, and it allows you to look at the list of what is running, and at the bottom right, you also get the option of the new desktop, and that can make your life so much easier.

Touchpad Gestures

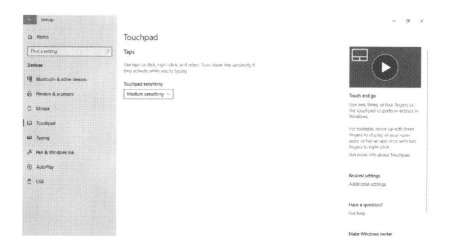

 If you have a touch, compatible computer, this can also make your life a lot easier. If you are viewing every single open Window, you can swipe up in order to show the task view that you have. If you want to show the desktop once more, you take three fingers on the touchpad, and then swipe them down. If you want to swipe between different open Windows, place the three fingers onto the touchpad, and from there, swipe from right to left in order to toggle the controls on this. Ti's a good way to multitask without getting bogged down by Windows, since it can make everything so much better, and easier for you as a result, and for many people, these touchpad gestures can helps with improving the overall efficiency of the ability to use Windows 10.

Scrolling Inactive Windows

Sometimes, if you have a secondary Window that has a lot of data, you may want to scroll this. It will now allow you to scroll these Windows without switching to them, and it is a mouse trick that can inevitably help you. What you do is go to settings, and then deice, and from there mouse, and you will find the scroll inactive Windows when I hover over them feature, allowing you to toggle them to turn them on. Using the mouse, you will need to get the pointer over there, and from there you will notice that scrolling will work, and you can get all of the access to the secondary Window there, allowing you to multitask with Windows 10 in an effective manner.

There is another fun trick as well, and essentially, it has to click the space that is all the way in the lower right-hand concern, and that is right near where the date and time is. Once you do that, it can actually hide and sow the desktop. While it is not one that you need to automatically put in, you will definitely want to consider this especially if you're looking to have a better time with Windows 10, and if you're working with multiple desktops.

Mini Player

Finally, we have mini player, which is a great feature for those of us who love to watch videos at work, and it is great if you are working alone most of the time. You'll notice when you go to Windows 10 movies and TV, in the app there is a mini view option, which allows for you to have it be in the right-hand corner of the computer and this is good if you want to watch something, but don't feel like having it all right there. When your'e done with what your'e doing, you can always resize it back to normal as well.

22

With Windows 10, multitasking has never been easier, and even if you don't feel like using a billion different shortcuts, there is a lot that you can do with Windows 10, and a lot that is possible, so it's worth checking out as well if your'e thinking about doing a bunch with Windows 10, and want to easily, and without fail, create the best experience that you can with this..

Chapter 4 – Windows 10 Home Vs. Windows 10 Pro

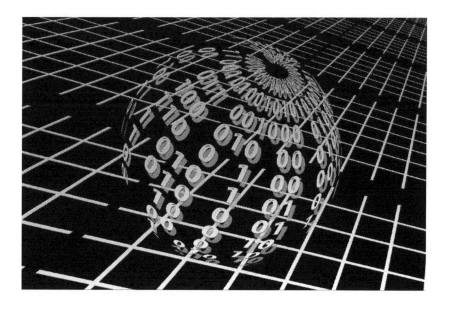

So maybe you have been on the fence about getting Windows 10 because there are two different options. Do you need the pro version? Do you need the home version? We will dive into what each of them has, and why you may want one over the other.

All about Windows 10 home

Windows 10 home has a few less features, but it definitely has a lot of features, more than 7 and 8.1 did. Home is the basic version of

Windows 10, and it comes with the revamped tart menu, and also comes with a disc operating system, Cortana assistant, and the features that everyone loves, such as battery saver, Windows Hello for biometrics and security, and TMP support. Bater saver is a great one to make your machine more power efficient by limiting the background apps being used. TPM allows for additional security, and many motherboard manufacturers have TPM in their device, and is your motherboard has that chip; Windows 10 home will support this. It also comes with everything that you want with Windows 10 home, such as virtual desktops, snap assist, and there is even continuum, which lets you have the switch from desktop in order to go to tablet mode. This also comes with Edge, but that is obvious. It also can get updates immediately and Microsoft Passport for extra security. This is a good one for those users at home that want something simple, yet effective.

Windows 10 home is also a little bit cheaper, but it honestly is not that giant of a price change, especially since it is about 80 dollars. You can get Windows 10 for home for 98 dollars on amazon now, whereas pro is 110 dollars these days on amazon. You may have to watch out though, because some of the cheap ones may give you dud activation key, so it might be best to get the retail versions, since there are not any upgrade versions that you have to worry about, like with the previous Windows 10 features.

Windows 10 Pro

Therefore, what do you get with Pro? Well, expect to have everything that the original home has, but there are a lot of other different data and disc encryption options as well, and there is group policy management, along with Client Hyper-V, which is a virtualization solution that you can get for Windows. If you are going to connect to a Windows domain for work, then I do suggest getting the pro version. If you are working with sensitive information, that does require a lot of encryption, then I do suggest getting the pro version. Otherwise, if you are just using this for your home computer that is not handling super secure data, then just get yourself a home version.

Now, we talked a little bit about the encryption. You have bit Locker on this, which essentially will allow people to fully secure the device and drives. Essentially, this is an all-or-nothing decision to fully encrypt the drive, and it allows for a bit more security, but at the risk of not being able to move files around. You can however, encrypt new files and then keep them around the unencrypted ones and they can be used just like USB sticks, so it will help with protecting the files.

There is also the remote desktop connection. Pro can only have the remote controlled ones. Home machines do have remote access, but it is many for an expert to show the home user some extra settings and they cannot do much more than that

There is also the group policy management and other features, all of which are on the pro version, and this also includes the business store. Microsoft also allows for people to join the Azure Active Directory, which allows a person to go to a bunch of cloud-posted apps that they can use. The support joining of the domain allows these PCs to be added to a full corporate network, but with Home, you genitally only get the Microsoft account, or rather than a local user function. So in essence, if you are using work and files that are encrypted and on certain services, you need to use Windows 10 pro in order to make a major difference. So yes, it is good if your're running this type of set of features for your business.

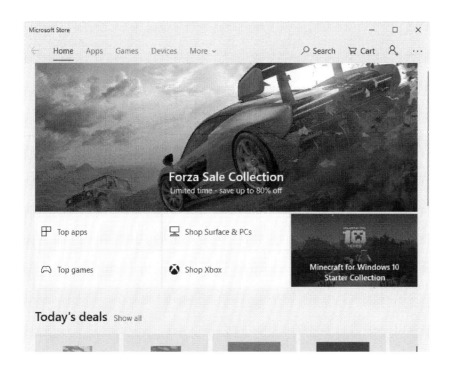

More than home and Pro

There are a few other options rather than home and pro, and they include enterprise and student. With enterprise, you can use this for corporations and organizations, and it comes with device guard to lock down devices. Enterprise is sold through a volume licensing though. The education one is used for schools and learning institutions, and it comes with the Enterprise features for the most part, but is also available through volume licensing. You can also get Windows 10 for smartphones, and it essentially uses the Windows 10 OPS for smartphones. There is also the Windows 10 core, which is good for IoT devices. Essentially, you can always do what you want with these, and you can choose the one that will provide the options that you need. If you are an institution, I suggest getting pro or enterprise, depending on what you need.

Regardless of what you get though, these are your typical features of Windows devices, and there is a lot that this has to offer. If you have been curious about what types of Windows systems will work best for you, as a general rule, those machines that are used for a business usually do better with just the home edition, whereas those that are businesses should consider pro options.

Chapter 5 – Navigating the Start Menu, Desktop, and Data Storage

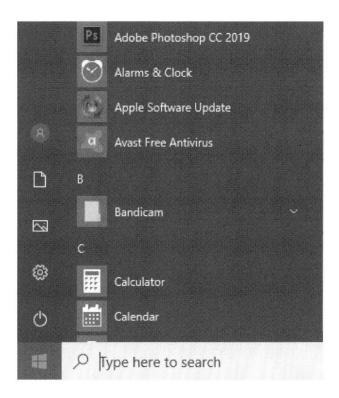

Therefore, you have chosen to get Windows 10, but when you look at it, it is just completely confusing. Well guess what, you are not alone! Here, we will discuss how you navigate the start menu, the desktop, and data storage.

The Start Menu

First, you have the desktop start menu. You have probably seen this start menu, where you press a button, and you are given a graphic, your username, and a place for the password. It is what will greet you when you turn the machine on, and once you unlock it, you will be able to then use it.

When you first open it up, you will see a lock screen. This essentially serves the purpose to well, lock the computer so that people don't get into your system, and you'll be able to when you look at this, get a quick rundown of your device and anything you need such as the time, date, your Wi-Fi strength, and sometimes even the weather. It also provides the batter y charge on your device as well. Sometimes, you can also get the downloads on your lock screen too. You do not really need all of that unless you want it. It is essentially, where you begin when you start, and it does give you the ability to answer Skype messages, or access the camera without fully logging in too, which is pretty neat.

From this point, you will want to log in. logging in basically tells the device "hey, this is me. Let me in!" so that you can use this. Personally, some people are okay with just a click to log in. If the computer doesn't' have sensitive information on this, you should be fine, but otherwise, for the sake of your own personal security, do yourself a favor and put a password on this.

Now, when you log in, you have three different ways, which are the touch screen to swipe a finger to go to the touch screen login, and from there the mouse to click and open up, and from there, you also have the keyboard, which with any key; you will be able to access this. Then, you officially log in by pressing the keys to type in the password. When you press OK, it will then let you in. That is all it takes!

Now, what is cool about this is that with logging in, you have a bunch of new ways to do it. Back in the day, it was just putting a password in. but you can do it in so many other ways including looking at your screen if you have Real Sense infrared cameras that recognize the face, swip8ng the fingers or even just pressing a button for your fingerprint, putting your eye up if you have eye recognition, drawing circles, lines or taps, or just using a PIN. You can always skip this too, especially if you feel like you do not need this, but I do not suggest doing that. That can spell trouble for you in the future.

So you have logged in. congrats! Now, you are onto the next part, and here, we will discuss the start menu and everything about that.

The Start menu

When you first log in, you will see a bar right down the bottom. That is the task bar. You can pin applications to this bar in order to make sure that you can easily access them. If you do not like that, you will then just press the Windows key, or simply chose start, and from there, you are at the start menu.

So you have the start menu here, and from this point, you will see all of the applications here, and from there, you go to all of them and see an alphabetical list of every single thing installed on there. You can also choose to search, typing in what you need, and Windows will bring this up. If you want to as well, you can always pin applications to the start menu. For example, if you use the Edge browser a lot, throwing that on these works. This will also give you the store, weather and traffic, and even Skype calls if you want to quickly access this, which is definitely a nice option.

If you want to realize this, you actually can, and that is because you have a whole bunch of the tiles that are there. While you cannot disable the tiles and anything, you can resize this. To resize, you move it over towards the Edge, and from there, click and drag. This in essence will give you more or less space. You will want to consider more space if you like to have a lot of live tiles. You usually with the smallest setting can get three columns of these tiles, but at max, it can handle size at a time. This is something that you can also change to make it look like it is like the Windows 8 screen, a and that is by right clicking the empty portion of the desktop, choose personalize, and from there, switch from use start full screen and from there, It'll be on. You will be able to get the live tiles to be on the entire desktop, which is handy if your'e using a touchscreen device.

Personalizing the Desktop

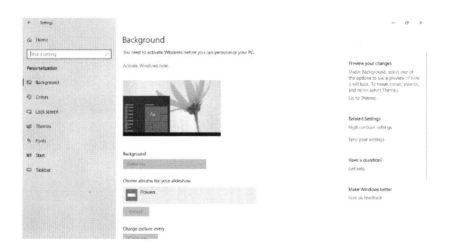

At this point, you can also personalize the desktop and the start menu, and you can do this by going to settings, and choosing desktop, and from there, monkeying around with the settings on this. You also can clutter up everything with icons that you need, but did you know that you could personalize the start menu. Go to start, and you can toggle to show the most used apps, the recently added ones, the full screen, or show what recently opened items on your lists are there. From there, you can choose t toggle these on or off on the tart menu.

You also can at this point, choose which folders you want to appear on the start menu, and you can enable or disable the file explorer link on the settings menu, along with any folders from this, including primary account folders, personal documents, any downloads, and the like. Going back on the backspace and from there choosing colors will allow you to choose the colors that you want for your Windows 10 start menu, which can look good or jarring depending on what you choose. You should inevitably choose one that best fits your device, and one that does not look too jarring to see. By changing this, you can have fun with this. You can also customize the taskbar too, not just the desktop background, and you can always choose to change this as you see fit.

Live Tiles

Live tiles are similar to the Windows 8 version, with a few differences with these tiles, you can drag and drop these wherever, and it can be rearranged, named, or deleted, and it does include the "life at a glance" and the "play and explore" options, and these are two default ones. You can however, using the mouse, hover over the tile, and click on the two bars that appear on the left, allowing you to edit, or remove these. You can always add new ones by clicking with a right click on the App Apps part of the start menus that is located on the Windows Explorer, and from here, choose to pin to the start menu. You can do apps, folders, or files on there and they will be their own tile. The tiles are mostly just shortcuts, but some of the universal Windows apps have a special type of live tile that's animated, and it's like a smartphone widget, but it works in the live tile area, such as weather, sports, and news, and you can even ad or disable animations simply by right clicking it and then turning it off.

Navigating Storage

Storage on Windows 10 provides features you may not be used to. You can get to it super easily though, and that's literally by typing into the search menu "storage" but if you want to do it in a way that's traditional, go to settings, then system, and then storage. You'll notice when you first get there that it is just describing all of the drives, the data that you've used on them, and the free space that's left. However, by clicking on them you open up other options, including a chance to dive deeper into what is eating up the disc space, and what you do not need.

If you are using this to clear out some more space on there, you want to first head to the C drive, also called "this PC" and from there, you want to bring up the Storage Usage Window, where you can see where most of the data is located. You will notice several sections here, including the system and reserves, documents, and apps and games, and you can from here click on this to find out where your data is being used, and from there, you will be able to delete as needed. "System and reserved" is where most of the data is, but, if you are not sure on how to tackle this part, do be careful.

One of the top files to give you more data is hibernation. If you never worry about hibernating your device, then disable this, and you will free up a lot immediately. You can also turn off the system restore if needed, but here is the thing about that: if you know there is a chance you might lose your data, do not turn this off. This can cause backups to be lost forever, and it will wipe everything, even though you may have a chance to restore it, you will lose all of your files. So remember that.

Removing Temporary Files

These are other files that you can move, and this is from the initial C drive menu, where you can scroll down to find downloads, temporary files, and the recycle bin. These are usually just files that you will want to get rid of, and you can always toss these. The recycle bin is another one that you can clear out as well. Downloads usually, if you do not have important files at this point, can be removed too, and you should definitely be smart with his. However, looking through, seeing the files that you have, and removing them can certainly help.

File Explorer

Finally, if you are looking for a certain file, why not try file explorer. This is something you can open up straight from the start menu, or just by typing in file explorer into the search bar, and from there, you'll get a whole set of different locations, including documents, downloads, pictures, and desktop. If you cannot find that, you can always go to the search bar and type in some keywords to help it search for this. This is a handy place, especially if your'e struggling to find a file for something important.

With the way the Windows 10 OS looks, you will definitely want to learn how to use this effectively, and with the right options, you will be much better off. With this, you can easily get a feel for how to use this OS, and in turn, you will be much better with the results of your actions, and you will be able to navigate this effectively.

Chapter 6 – How to Manage Files, programs, and Applications

We touched a little bit on this in the previous section, but here, we are going to tackle how you can manage your files, applications, and programs in Windows 10. with the changes made to file explorer and the like, it is no wonder why people are using this more and more. Here, we will touch on how to manage all of these, and what that can mean for you as a person that uses Windows 10.

File Explorer

This is your first option, and you can literally click the file at the very bottom, or just go to the taskbar and choose start, and then file explorer. At this point, you will see a whole bunch of options here, including quick access. This used to be called favorites, but you will be able to see all of the folders and files that you have created and you can access easily.

File explorer can be used for a lot of different reasons, including to management of your files and folders, along with internal storage, attached storage, and even optical drives. For example, you can use the navigation bar to find some of the different options in this, especially if you are looking for a file that you cannot seem to find. Quick access is good for your most accessed files and folders that you have pinned, and that is a new option for Windows 10

We also have the ribbon toolbar, which we are going to touch on in the next section.

The Ribbon Toolbar

The ribbon toolbar is essentially one menu that has a bunch of tabs that are always there, along with contextual tabs, which show up as you type in anything within the search bar. This is good and it is designed to look for up to 200 different file management commands. The ribbon menu showcases the file, home, share, and view options. The file menu is essentially made to give you access to the greater commends that you get with file explorer. This includes opening up a new Window, command prompt, and even options, and usually, this is when you want to enter new programming commands.

The file menu also allows you to open up new explorer Windows too, and it is good as well for changing search and folder options, and if you need help, this is where help is. The Home menu allows for you to manage the files. Clipboard has all of the standard commands, including copy and paste, which is great if your'e trying to organize all of this.

With the home menu, you can move to, copy, move to a new group, and even delete and rename files in this group. You will then be able to move the files with a new group, or even easy access and you will then be able to map out everything. There are also open, along with edit commands, which are good if you want to quickly open something. Not only that, there is also file history, and in turn, it will allow you to monitor the files that are stored in the libraries, favorites, desktop, and contacts, and it allows you to make changes to what you need, provide backups, and the like.

The share tab is essentially, how you share with others, where you share to a contact group that is already there, and create zip files to email, or burn it to discs, or even just print or fax the documents. You will be amazed at how you can share all of this, and it is an advanced security tab that allows you to lock down the sharing as well.

Finally, you have the view tab, which allows you to configure how you want to display the files. You can configure the navigation panes, and from there disable or enable the previews, and from there, you can choose the layout of all of this, allowing you to choose how you can handle all of these files.

With the ribbon toolbar, it will make using file explorer much easier, and you will be able with this, to manage all of the files and programs you have in Windows 10

Other important Areas

There are a couple of other small places you should know about with Windows 10 that are different. First, you have OneDrive, where if you have this set up on a PC, if you put it in there, and it's all synched up, you can actually access this from another computer, simply by logging in. This is really good if you want to look at the different aspects of your system, and it can help.

You also have This PC bar. This is everything that is on your internal storage, and this includes optical media. If you are looking to manage the apps that you have, and other files that are not word documents or documents period, I suggest going to this. p 9

Finally, you've got the status bar, which showcases the information that is there about files that are stored, including the number of files, the size, the file selection, a and quick access to the layout of folders, again another helpful addition.

Managing Apps in Windows 10

If you have apps that you would like to have enabled or disabled, you essentially always go to settings then apps, and then choose the app, you would like to manage permissions from, and then click on the advanced options link that is there. At this point, you will be able to manage a number of settings about the apps, and the settings for these that are there from the Microsoft store may not have as many setting permissions as you would like.

For programs that you want to uninstall, you literally go to this and choose the app that is there. It should give you the option to uninstall, unless it is from the Microsoft store. Choose that, and you will get a popup that you want to confirm. From there, by simply confirming it, you will be able to uninstall the app, and from there, make your life so much easier with time.

With Windows 10, managing your files, apps, and games has never been easier, and here, you learned some of the key features that can be used to help make this easier as well.

Chapter 7—Using Microsoft Edge

Microsoft Edge is been something that lots of people have not always liked. But Edge has changed a lot as of late, and here, we will talk about how you can use Microsoft Edge in order to really get a feel for some of the features. To begin, you press the Edge icon, and you can work with this, but we will also give you some tis and how to use Microsoft Edge to the best that it can be.

To Begin

Once Edge is launched, you are going to see the MSM apps, and from there, you will see the start menu and Cortana sorts of features, with the rotating tiles and news pieces. There is a customize link that is up on the right, and you can highlight up to six topics on there. It definitively is pretty simple. Our launch a new tab and you will see the icons of the frequently visited sites, and the search bar that are there. You use the Bing search engine by default, which is equal to google in many regards, and once you put it there in, Bing can hunt it down. From there, it can swap the home screen for its own, and Microsoft chooses what you look at, and you can choose that too. You will probably know about this, but the upper left has the back and forward arrows, and the loop icon in order to reload pages. Once you add an icon, it will be there. The search bar is located near the middle of the screen, and on the top right are a few other icons.

Navigation

navigating is pretty simple, and you just type in what you need to type in, choose your location, move forwards and backwards to the site itself, and from there, you can choose to ad favorites by clicking the star icon. Press the plus button on the header bar, or Ctrl+T in order to choose what you need to open. You can also chose to search privately by clicking the ellipsis in the menu on the upper right, and then launch the InPrivate session via the options. It will not hide the activity from the ISP or employer, but you will not have a browsing record on the PC.

There are a couple more things that you can do at this point, which is set up the homepage and import the bookmarks. You go to settings, and then advanced settings, from the top, you can toggle to show the home button, and once that is enabled, you add a homepage to this.

In addition, while you are here, you can choose between the light and dark themes that are there. If you are there already, you can also import your bookmarks and favorites, and you can from there, use the dropdown menu, and then export the file from C that has the name bookmarks in it. Copy it to Windows 10 and import it there. If that does not work, you may need to copy this. For chrome, it is just downloading it to the PC, which synchronizes these up, so if you choose to export form Edge, you will have it there, but you may need to rearrange this.

Other things you can do

There is so much that you can do with Microsoft Edge. For example, your reading list, which is the bookmark, can be something you add to. Whenever you do it, you can read the content offline, and you can do it without an internet connection. You can also write on the web with Microsoft Edge too.

Edge is the only browser that lets you take notes, highlight or doodle. To do this, you simply choose the option to add notes that is located in the options section, and from there, you can write what you want to write on. It has the ballpoint pen, highlighter, or even adding notes and sharing this. There are many different options, and it even includes highlighting and erasing notes, which is pretty impressive.

You can also identify what version of Edge you are using. This can happen in settings, and by going to about this App, you will figure out whether or not you are running the most current version, and if there are changes that you can make to achieve this.

Finally, if your'e worried about clearing data. You can always go to more, and then settings and you can choose the clear browsing data. You can have it clear everything out, or you can choose what to clear. You can choose what data you want to get rid of, and then choose it. if you feel like you want to use this to clear out something all the time, you can turn on the function of always clear when I close this browser setting, and just toggle that to on.

New Features

With Edge, Microsoft wants to add new features, because lots of people do not actually like Edge. They recently added new privacy controls, and under settings, you can choose whether to have unrestricted, balanced, or strict settings, and it allows for third parties to track your activity. The extent of this remains to be seen, but there are different ways to protect yourself. Businesses and internal sites are also using the collections feature, which is another good one that allows for people to collect, organize, and then export and from there share the content that they need, making it even better. There are also plans to customize the Chromium code, which have already been put in, but you should soon see more of this over time.

With new additions being made to Edge, this should get people to want to use this browser more and more. It is a good one, and it is definitely improved since the internet explorer days. Sometimes a little bit of rebranding can help, and in this, you learned how you can get the most out of Microsoft Edge that you possibly can.

Chapter 8—Setting up and Maintaining Windows 10

Let us take a moment to talk about setting up, while also touching on how to perform maintenance with Windows 10 in a way that is effective, and can help you keep the system running up to snuff. Windows 10 is easy once you have the hang of it, but here, we will talk about how you can use the different features here in order to keep Windows 10 in proper order.

The Setup

First, you will need a stable internet connection, and from there, you will then start to be able to work with the setup. If you do not have Windows 10 already downloaded, or the disc inserted in there to install, you are going to need to add that. From here, you will want to make sure your device drivers are currently up to date. If you don't' have an Ethernet adaptor, or do not have network connection period, you will need that first and foremost.

You will also want to make sure your drivers are up to date. It is important to make sure that your system does not have in-box drivers that are out of date. You can always make sure that you have the system restore there, and from there, once that is on, you can configure, and choose to turn on system protection.

At this point, once you have set all of this up, you are going to need to put a Microsoft account in. If you already have one, then great, you just have to put that in, if not, you should create one. Why does it matter? Well, if you like to use OneDrive, files, and also store your Skype accounts or even get Cortana personalized, this can help. Sometimes though, if your'e trying to set it up fast, going with express settings is your best option. You can always do it with a local account as well, and you can always choose to fix this over time, especially if you want to add the professionalization later on.

At this point, you will be given a chance to set up your professionalization. For starters, you may want to determine whether you want Edge as the default browser. Some people are okay with this, since it now supports Last Pass, along with RoboForm password managers, but some people may want to use another type of browser. If you don' want to use Edge, you go to settings, then apps, and then default apps, and then, you set the defaults based on app, and you choose chrome, or whatever browser you want, and from there, you can set that as the default.

At this point, you can also personalize other aspects of this too. You may want to go to the "ease of access" section, which allows you to put narrator (which tells you what is on the screen) magnifier (which zooms in) or even the on-screen keyboard, any mouse points, or closed captions and subtitles, and you can toggle all of this as needed. You can choose all of this based on personal preference.

Next, you want to choose your privacy settings. There are a few settings that you can turn off and on to improve privacy, such as advertising ID, key logging, and speech recognition. You should also turn off feedback and diagnostics, which is where you control the data that is sent directly to Microsoft, and what will be sent with your ID. Again, choose to turn these off as needed, for it can be helpful

At this point, installing office 365 is your next option. You get a subscription for this costs about 70 dollars a year, and if you have multiple computers, you can also get the some option for a little bit more, which allows for the apps to be shared. There are free word processor alternatives, but usually, they are not as good as 365 is. If you already have the computer open, going to office.com can help you install this.

If you have to change anything else, do so, but the last part of this is the update schedule, and restoring your backups. Windows 10 will install the updates automatically, but if you want to defer or postpone them, you can go to update and security, and then choose Windows update to find out the updates. If there are some available, you can install them right then and there, or if you want to have them installed at another time, you simply just have it during the active hours.

Finally, you have to back this up. If you had everything on OneDrive already, sign in, and from there, you choose the synch this up. This is great, and there is also the files-on-demand feature that allows you to keep everything on the cloud, but still managed with file explorer. You right click the OneDrive function, and from there, go to settings, and then click the files-on-demand icon, choose to click it, and from there, you will be able to control everything. If you do need to install a backup on your files, you should always do this, but usually, this part is pretty simple.

And there you have it! Everything is neatly installed, and you will be able to, without many problems, utilize your system effectively, and without any problems, and in turn, create a better environment for your Windows 10 system.

Maintaining Windows 10

So you've set it up. That's great, but do you know how to maintain it? Here are some important Windows 10 maintenance tips.

First, clean out the junk files every so often. Depending on the usage, you could do it every week, or every month, and you can use the disc cleanup to help get rid of these junk files. This in turn will be cleared out, and allow for you to not have to worry about it sitting there clogging your device up.

Next, make sure that you have the latest updates for your device. I know updating isn't always fun, but here's the thing, sometimes, getting that update can help beef up the security, and by going to settings, updates and security, going to Windows update, and then checking for updates, you'll definitely want to get this. In addition, sometimes PCs will run slower if there are updates that need to be done, so keep that in mind as well.

Next, clean out the registry. Registry cleans are good, and they can help to get rid of any errors. Some people do not clean their registry, some do, and some people do not like the idea of cleaning the registry, since they used to leave orphaned entries there. But not anymore! Windows PCs run better if you do clean out the registry every so often, and get rid of the different errors that may be there. It also will help to make everything cleaner.

Sometimes, if you notice that your PC is running slow, it might need a restart. Windows 10 devices tend to mess up certain aspects, including sound on streaming services, and if you notice this problem, sometimes a good restart will help. At this point, when you restart this, do make sure that you're only keeping the apps that you want open, and do make sure that if there are files on there you don't need, or any apps that keep opening, try to disable them and prevent them from opening up all the time. For example, Skype is better just being left closed unless you need it, since it can slow down the computer.

Finally, on occasion, go to the control panel of your device, and then go to the applet that is called uninstall programs. You should look at all of the installed software there. You should make sure that everything that is on there is something that you have installed, since potentially unwanted programs may get onto there.

If you need to install a new program to try it out, always create a system restore point, and then install this. From there, you can determine if you want to keep it. If not, just uninstall and if needed, go back to the restore point.

You can also restrict the startups, since many times, you do not need to use this much at all. This is something you can decide of yourself too.

With Windows, understanding how to turn it on, run it, and from there, use it effectively, will help with improving your ability to use this, and over time, it can make a difference in how your PC runs.

Chapter 9—Accessing music, photos, and films with Windows 10

With Windows 10, you can access music, photos, and films easily. There are different apps you can use these days, all of which work to your own personal benefit. How? Well, read on to find out how you can access music, films, and photos with the use of Windows 10.

Accessing Photos

First, in order to access all of your photos, you can go to start, and then choose photos. There is also a photos app that you can get straight from Windows if you feel like this is something that you want to use.

With this, once you open this, you will be able to look at the photos by date, projects, album, or even people or folder. The app actually can recognize all of the faces that are there. For example, if you type in cat, you will get all the photos of cats. You can also upload photos initially, and this is simple by installing the OneDrive app, and from there, going to settings and turning on the function to camera upload, and it will all be on there.

Usually, for the most part, all images will be put in the pictures folder. Sometimes if you get them directly from the internet, you can go to the downloads folder, and it will all be there. The same goes for videos as well.

Music

Many people use other music services, but for Windows 10 users, you are kind of stuck with Groove music as a default music player. But, it is recently changed and Microsoft understands that you have other ways to stream music. For example, Spotify, will have it on there. Within the groove app, you get a one-click method to move everything that you need from Spotify over to groove music, so if you are going to move your music, you can. Nowadays, if you actually have a lot of music, the groove music app on Windows 10 will directly catalog, and then play it all for you, and it will tell you where to find this.

The app itself is pretty simple. You can actually go to settings and then music to figure out where you are going with this. For example, going to music on this PC, you will be able to from there look at the local music option to find you more about this. You can also have the app retrieve the missing artwork and the metadata as well, so if your'e a stickler for this, you can replace it all somewhere. You can also choose the background functions as well.

Videos

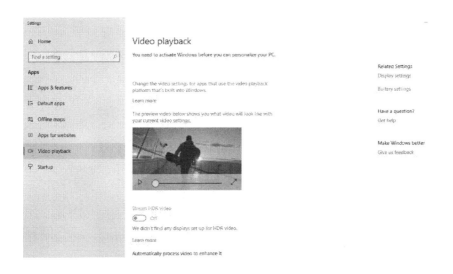

Finally, you have videos, which if you want to get the media player, you can always go through and look for this. If you are considering getting an app for this, media monkey is good. If you are looking to put together a library of different options, including the different folders, and universal plug and play, you can do that with this. Media monkey is good for those who are looking for a good means to really get the most that you can from your video playing, and by installing a video player, you can stream directly to Windows 10

With all of the different media players, you have a lot you can work with, and Windows 10 realizes this. Here, you are given a wide variety of different ways to stream your content, allowing for you to get the most that you can from Windows 10, and to effectively and, without fail, stream your favorite media from every device.

Chapter 10—Windows 10 troubleshooting

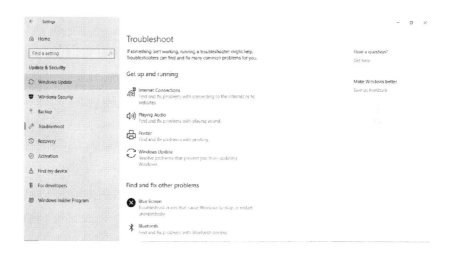

Windows 10 is a great system, but sometimes, you can have troubleshooting issues. Here are a few things you can do to fix common errors with Windows 10.

Issues with upgrading

This I a common issue for those that have it happen when they first install from 7 or 8, and usually it's the get Windows app error saying that the machines here aren't compatible, and it wasn't appearing, or stalled and failed downloads. A few things that you can do is to make sure that the PC itself is up to date. You will need to make a media creation tool if you cannot get it fixed otherwise. You should make sure that the hardware disable execution prevention is switch over to bios, and if you still have issues, search for performance in the start menu, and from there, you can upgrade to the latest Windows 10 version.

Windows 10 Freezing

This is something that a few people have struggled with, but there are a few ways to fix it. First, use the recovery console, where you restart your PC, and when you get there, you hold the shift key and then restart. You then want to go to troubleshoot, advanced options, and then go to a previous build. If you do not have this option, you will need to use the settings app in safe mode. You will want to make sure to select either 4 or F4 in order to start the PC in safe mode. Go to settings. and then go to update and security, and from there, you can go back to an earlier build. For the most part though, usually a restart will fix your Windows 10 machine.

Less Storage Than Before

This is a problem with some people when they install Windows 10 and realize they have a lot less space. This is because you typically have both the new OS and the previous OS on there. The solution to that is pretty simple, and that is to go to cleanup, and you can have it automatically clean this up. You should see the drive box, and from there, select the drive the OS is on and the default drive should appear initially. If you are confident that this is the drive that you want to have, then press OK and Windows will find this. You'll also want to, at this point once it's finished going through everything, find the one that says "previous Windows version" on it. From there, if it is there, you will then want to delete that. You also may want to clean up the system files, and you will be given the option to delete the previous installations. It could take up to 5GB of storage, and from there, press OK, and in another message, you can ask if you want to send this. From there, choose to delete files and then they are complete.

Can't Play DVDs

This is actually a feature, rather than a glitch. This is a strange thing, but Microsoft actually does not allow you to launch the current OS without a media player. You can get the DVD player app, which is a little bit expensive, but if you did upgrade 10 from 7 or 8.1, you should have a free option for this, which is pretty cool.

Issues with Memory

This is another common performance issue, and it relates to something that is called virtual memory. The OS is a little bit stingy with this, and if you do not' have RAM, it can cause issues. The solution to this is simple, and that has to go to control panel, type in performance, and from there, choose to adjust the appearance along with the performance of Windows. Choose the advanced tab, and then go to virtual memory in terms of section. Uncheck the "automatically manage paging file size for the drives" section, and then choose the drive that contains the Windows 10 files, whether that be C or otherwise. Choose custom size, and then add initial and maximization sizes. By pressing OK, and then restarting, you can fix these settings.

Turning off Forced updates

Then there are the forced updates. This is something that a lot of users do not like, and while you do get the option to postpone these now, and choose when to get them, you may not want to deal with this period. It is better to deal with this when it has gotten the kinks fixed, the workaround for pro users is to use the group policy editor, and you can navigate to the Windows update within the components, Windows, and the administrative templates. You can double click to configure the update, and then enable the radio button, and from there, you can have it notify you as well whenever there is an installation. This is a good thing for those who want to wait on it, but the one problem is that if you are using the Windows defender system, this can become a super annoying thing.

Since group policy editor is not available in Windows 10, but you can go to Windows update in the updates and security feature. You can from there choose the advanced options, and then choose to notify to schedule restart, and once you are there, you can also choose how the updates get delivered, so that you are getting them on the local networks.

Turning off notifications You Don't Need

Windows 10 has an action center that is a great way to view the messages and notifications from pretty much everything that you need. But, it becomes super annoying once you get messages that you don't' care about, or repeated messages that get annoying to read every single time. But, there is a way to ensure that you are only getting the relevant information from the action center. What you do, is you go to settings, then system, then notifications and actions. You are going to see a whole lot of apps and ways notifications are shown, so you can turn off and turn on different notifications. You can turn off Windows tips, and even disable the notifications that show up within the lock screen, and you can also disable these n a per-app basis, so if you're sick of something telling you to update, you can simply turn those off.

Files Opening in Wrong Apps

This is another annoying one, especially if you do not want to use that app. This is because you did not change the default apps for some files Windows 10 sets those associations to the default, but you may want to put them to something else. It is not hard though. You right-click the file that is opening wrongfully, and go to "open with" and then choose a different app. You then choose your app, and choose to always use that app. Bam, problem solved.

Troubleshooting Windows 10 is not all that hard, and you will be able to, with this, create a better result with your Windows 10 experience, and in turn, fix some of the major bugs that are there.

Chapter 11—The most important Windows 10 Apps You Should Know

Windows 10 has a lot of great apps and features that can help you a whole lot. Here are the features you should know about, and why they matter, including a few tips for each.

Ninite for Windows 10

One of the best apps you can get is Ninite for Windows 10. This allows you to put all of the different apps that you want on there immediately. You can install the apps within their default location, without the extra junk, and if you have a 64-bit machine, it will handle all of that. It also will put the apps on there, and also prevent the reboot requests from installers. You can get all of these with proxy settings too from Edge. You can also download all of these apps immediately, and save you time. This is a great one for file sharing, compression, other utilities, and even developer tools including python and other coding options, making coding so much more possible.

Ninite handles all of the updates at once, and it will help you pick the apps you want to install, and to update, and from there you go.

Recuvea

Have you ever deleted a file you wish you had access to once again? Well, Recuvea can help with that. It's an undeletion program for Windows 10 machines, and it's freemium. It allows you to undelete files that you have deleted, and it marks where on the disk they were stored and they are put there. This can recover everything from memory cards, media players, flash drives, and even hard drives. It's a great way to salvage some of the files that you might've mistakenly deleted, and it has an effective means to recover. The only time it does not is when the operating system has new data that is written over the deleted file, which means it's not possible.

Speccy

Are you curious about your Windows 10 specs? If you've been wondering this, including both the hardware and the software, then Speccy is for you. It's another Freemium app that you can put on there, and it will tell you the brand and model of the processor, the hard drive speed and size, the amount of RAM on it, graphics card information, and also the operating system, and it will tell you important information about the hardware. It is very clean and detailed, and it will give you good system information so that you can gather important info, and do it quickly, and it will help provide the technical details, and it's pretty good for those who need that information as well. It is being updated constantly to cater to Windows 10 as well.

Process explorer

This is another free software that is essentially task manager but even more in-depth. It can help to collect information about the processes on the system, and is great for debugging software and system problems. It can help with searching for resources that are held by processes and other processes that may be holding it back. It also can show the command lines used in a program, especially helpful for identifying the processes that you need. It also shows what is maxing out CPU, and it will also give you lots of information to help you find the processes holding your machine back.

LastPass

Lastpass is one of the best ways to help save all your passwords. It is now on Edge as well, and you can download this directly from the Windows store in order to help you really get your passwords all saved.

Lastpass will save all of the passwords that you use on the browser itself, and from there, you can securely access your sites without having to remember troublesome passwords. This is great for every mobile device and computer, and it helps especially if you work with a ton of sites, and do not want to deal with the trouble of saving passwords.

Spotify

Yes, Spotify is great for Windows 10. You can get it downloaded from the Windows store, and is supported in over 60 different countries, and it works in the same way as the Win32 application. You can share the songs that you want to whenever, or wherever you want, and it also will allow you to share and make the playlists that you want, and Spotify can even suggest some great music for you. You can get free options, or even the premium option that allows for you to take the music in offline fashions

Wunderlist

Do you use your computer enough to have everything neatly on a list? Well, why not try Wunderlist. You can actually use this with your phone, Alexa, or whatever you want to keep track of. It allows you to manage tasks you need to get done, and it also has smartwatch compatibility. It is free, and there is a paid version, but usually, for basic lists, it is good. It is got over 13 million users, and it is a good one if you are not a fan of the to-do option that is being integrated into office 365. It allows you to create tasks, get details on them, and also get you to find out any details on them, including when they're done, and it will even put subtasks on there too!

Ccleaner

This is a great way to clean out your computer. It is a way to clean out the unwanted files, including temporary files from the internet, and it uses code to do this. If you have invalid registry entries on Windows or other things that are clogging up your device, this is a great option to use. It is one of the best cleaners, and it has been used ever since 2004, so it does work. It can clean out any of the files from programs that you have, and it can also uninstall programs that you do not need anymore, including install files, and it can delete restore points if you want that.

Unlocker & LockHunter

Lockhunter is a great one for those pesky files that Windows won't let you delete. It allows you to remove files and folders that file explorer won't let you delete. It's a great one that's been around for almost a decade, and it's good for those rare moments when Windows refuses to let you manipulate files due to programs not letting you get access, this is important especially if somehow a virus or the like gets on there. It's good to keep around for a rainy day.

Unlocker pretty much does the same thing, and is another good one. This one allows you to delete files that are locked, and you will be able to get past those messages that say that you cannot delete the file, or access is denied. There is even a portable option, but it does not contain the delta toolbar, like how the desktop version does.

Paint 3D

Finally, we've got Paint 3D, which is a creative app that's used for Windows 10 only, and it's a small, but powerful tool that allows you to combine the paint and 3D options. It is a great one for basic design experience, and with just learning the ropes, you will get it. For example, learning all of the different brushes and how they work will allow you to provide a personalized design that works for the creation you are trying to make.

You can from here start to draw 2D shapes, and from there, create circles with the right angles that you have, and from there, you can then bring it to the Remix community, and there is even a forum that allows you to put the 3D and 2D shapes together, which is pretty cool.

Windows 10 has some amazing apps, and you can use all of these to get the full benefits that are possible. With the right apps, you will have success, and with the tools you have, there is a lot that Windows has to offer, so definitely take advantage of it when possible.

Chapter 12—Microsoft Office and Microsoft Intune

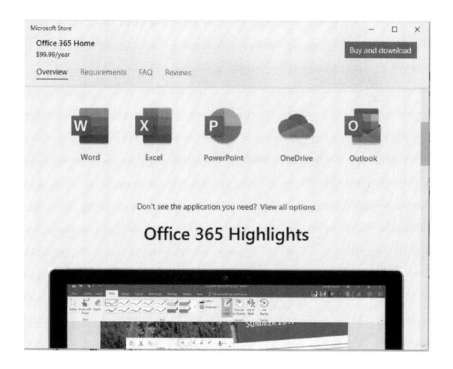

Finally, let us touch a little bit on both Microsoft office, and Microsoft Intune. This is a set of great systems that you can use to help you as a business professional do so much more, and here, we will discuss the ins and outs of both of these, and why they matter.

Microsoft office

Microsoft office at the core are all of the different products and applications that can be used in the office. Word documents, that you use in Microsoft word, are a part of this, but you also have Excel which handles spreadsheets, PowerPoint for presentations, and Microsoft outlook, all of which will help you with using this all in the office.

We will go over each of them below.

First, you have word, which is the word processor that we all know if you have ever written anything, chances are, 99% of the time your'e using Microsoft word. But, you can use it for papers, notes, calendars, resumes, and even brochures. It comes with a spelling and grammar checker, and you can even export different files, and it is pretty good for anyone working with this system.

Next, you got excel, which handles spreadsheets, doing calculations, boasting graphics and other analysis options, and it is pretty much how you create spreadsheets. You can collaborate in this as well, which is something that you probably like.

Powerpoint is something that, if you have ever done any presentation in school within the last 20 years, you know about this. You probably spent way too much time working with the text and transitions and the like. It allows you to create presentations, along with images, graphics, texts, and videos and animations, along with notes. It is great because you can collaborate on these as well, and you can get multiple people to work with you at the same time.

You also have OneNote, which is essentially, where all of the ideas and such can be organized into one central location, where you can type, make tables, insert links and pictures, and even do graphics. But, the big difference is that all of this is untethered, so you can pretty much put anything you want on there. It is similar to Evernote if you know that one, and it is pretty good. There might be some restraints, especially for page size, arrangement, and structure, but it is a great way to pretty much throw all of the notes that you have into one centralized location.

You have OneDrive too, which as we have mentioned before is a cloud drive that allows you to share and collaborate files that you want. You can store and access files from these devices and folder that you can share publicly, or specifically selected if you have office 365 immediately, you will get this for free, but if you want more than 5GB, you will need the subscription service.

Finally, you have ~~publisher~~ OUTLOOK, and you will want to consider using this if you have a bit of scheduling issues. It is pretty much an email service for people, and its part of the office suite of products that you can use for email. It also allows you to look at contacts, calendar, and files, so you can stay connected.

You also get the Skype for Business app with all of this. While it is its own separate application, if you are not using it for business, you can actually get it as a business app within the suite of products, which is cool.

You also have Microsoft publisher, which allows you to pretty much design anything that you need, including greeting cards, professional newsletters, and the like, and from there, you can publish and send it out for even more fun, and to bring forth the different applications for this. It allows you to pretty much do everything in one centralized location.

Finally, you have Microsoft access, which is a way to pretty much look at data and manage it. You get new charts with the upgrade, and you will be able to understand the data that you get, along with the reports that you also get from this too. You can match the chart dimensions to the fields, and from there preview the changes immediately. You can look at the way categories are displayed, along with the vertical access, including the Y values, in the proper manner. It is the perfect data visualization program for those that need it.

Microsoft Intune

This is one of the newer programs that is a cloud-based program for mobility management of different enterprises, in order to help keep everyone in the corporate locations productive. If you know about Azure services, this is actually a great one and it does come with the Azure portal too. With this, you can manage the mobile devices and the PCs in the office in order to access the company data, and from there, manage any apps that the workforce does use. It does allow for you to protect the company information, in order to help prevent anyone who should not be accessing this from accessing it. Finally, it allows for devices to be compliant with the company security needs and requirements.

It is essentially a part of the enterprise mobility and security suite that allows for it to fully integrate with the Azure Active Directory, in order to identify and control the access of the this information. When you use this, you can enable the workforce to be productive on these devices, while keeping the information that is there protected. It allows you to have good device management of different devices, such as if you are working in POS systems, you can have this all be controlled by this and have the tablets controlled by this service. It also allows you to have app management and data protection if you want your workforce to access different data and devices, and you will be able to really any of the technology on this, and it will allow you to see what people are doing.

It is great since you can enroll these devices in IT management, and configure this so that it meets the standards of the company, and you can get a VPN for these devices too. It is great for corporations that want to make sure some secure data is protected.

With the way the Microsoft applications work to help others get the most that they can, both Microsoft office and Intune are helpful with this. You can, with this service, actually help to keep the entire office on track, and to prevent any snags in the office. if you don't need this right away, that's fine, just remember that if you're considering potentially having your entire office on board with a singular function, and to help keep everyone in check, then let Microsoft help with this, and you'll be able to do so much with these Windows application.

Conclusion

Microsoft services, including Windows 10, have helped many people improve their lives, and in turn, create a better, more rewarding situation. It allows for people to have a seamless experience with their Microsoft products, and in turn, you will be able to get a better result from this as well. Choosing to use Microsoft services is helpful, and Windows 10 is a great upgrade. It is past the days where it is a problem, where bugs are a big issue with the system, but instead, it is a seamless system, and a good OS for your computer.

If you have not upgraded to Windows 10 just yet, and want to at this point, then you should. Windows 10 is a great OS, and you will be able to, with it, really take your computer to the next level. For those people that want to really get the most out of their Windows OS, and to really customize it, or if you are, someone that feels that they need to start using Windows 10 more and more, then you should definitely consider trying out everything that is here. It is pretty simple, and installation and all of the different features have made the process more seamless.

So your next step, one that you should definitely consider doing, is to make sure that you have the right OS on there. If you are upgrading from Windows 8 or 7 to 10, then do so, and from there, you can start to net all of the great benefits of the Windows 10 system. There is a lot that you can do with this, and if you are struggling with figuring out Windows 10 and all of the features, you can always come back to this guide.

Windows 10 is getting better and better, and with the new May release and the new build, you'll be able to take your Windows 10 machine to the next level, and it's even got so good that Edge is a browser that people can use, and one that can get a lot of great results.

I hope, that you really enjoyed reading my book.

Thanks for buying the book anyway!

Made in the USA
Monee, IL
19 September 2019